D0547536

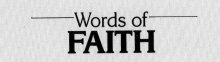

Words of
FAITH

Copyright © 1974 Lion Publishing

Published by
Lion Publishing plc
Icknield Way, Tring, Herts, England
ISBN 0 85648 304 4
Albatross Books
PO Box 320, Sutherland, NSW 2232, Australia
ISBN 0 86760 214 7

First edition 1974, under the title *A Song of Faith*
Reprinted 1975, 1976, 1977, 1980, 1981, 1982,
1983, 1984 (twice), 1985

Photographs by Lion Publishing/David Alexander

Quotations from *Good News Bible*, copyright 1966,
1971 and 1976 American Bible Society; published
by Bible Societies/Collins

Printed and bound in Hong Kong

Words of
FAITH

THE LORD MY SHEPHERD

The Lord is my shepherd;
I have everything I need.
He lets me rest in fields of green grass
and leads me to quiet pools of fresh water.
He gives me new strength.
He guides me in the right way,
as he has promised.
Even if that way goes through deepest
darkness,
I will not be afraid, Lord,
because you are with me!
Your shepherd's rod and staff keep me safe.

You prepare a banquet for me,
where all my enemies can see me;
you welcome me by pouring ointment on my
head
and filling my cup to the brim.
Certainly your goodness and love will be
with me as long as I live;
and your house will be my home for ever.

PSALM 23

An Eastern shepherd leads his sheep in the hills of
Judea.

ALL DAY LONG I TRUST IN YOU

To you, Lord, I offer my prayer;
in you, my God, I trust.
Save me from the shame of defeat;
don't let my enemies gloat over me!
Defeat does not come to those who trust in
you,
but to those who are quick to rebel against
you.

Teach me your ways, Lord,
make them known to me.
Teach me to live according to your truth,
because you are my Saviour.
All day long I trust in you.

From PSALM 25

Two donkey-riders on a track through the stony
landscape of southern Israel.

AT NIGHT, A QUIET MIND

There are many who say,
'How we wish to receive a blessing!'
Look on us with kindness, Lord!
The joy that you give me is much greater
than the joy of those who have plenty of
grain and wine.

As soon as I lie down, I go quietly to sleep;
You alone, Lord, keep me perfectly safe.

From PSALM 4

Mediterranean breakers reflect the setting sun.

I WAKE UP SAFE

You, Lord, always shield me from danger;
you give me victory
and restore my courage.
I call to the Lord for help,
and from his sacred hill he answers me.

I lie down and sleep,
and I wake up safe, because the Lord
protects me.
I am not afraid of the thousands of enemies
who surround me on every side.

From PSALM 3

A gazelle at Ein Gedi, where David hid from his
enemies.

GOD'S PROMISES

'But now I will come,' says the Lord,
  'because the needy are oppressed,
  and the persecuted groan in pain.
  I will give them the security they long for!'
The Lord's promises can be trusted;
  they are as genuine as silver,
  refined seven times in the furnace.

From PSALM 12

Light at the end of a dark tunnel in the ruins of the
Roman theatre at Miletus.

NEW CONFIDENCE

I love the Lord, because he hears me;
he listens to my prayers.
He listens to me
every time I call to him.
Death drew its ropes tight round me,
the horrors of the grave closed in on me;
I was filled with fear and anxiety.
Then I called to the Lord,
'I beg you, Lord, save me!'

The Lord is merciful and good;
our God is compassionate.
The Lord protects the helpless;
when I was in danger, he saved me.
Be confident, my heart,
because the Lord has been good to me.

From PSALM 116

Guy-ropes on a bedouin tent in the desert.

I WILL NOT BE AFRAID

The Lord is my light and my salvation;
I will fear no one.
The Lord protects me from all danger;
I will not be afraid.

When evil men attack me and try to kill me,
they stumble and fall.
Even if a whole army surrounds me,
I will not be afraid;
even if my enemies attack me,
I will still trust God. . .

In times of trouble he will protect me in his
shelter;
he will keep me safe in his temple,
and place me securely on a high rock.
So I will triumph over my enemies round me.
With shouts of joy I will offer sacrifices in
his temple;
I will sing, I will praise the Lord!

From PSALM 27

A lighthouse at the port of Jaffa, ancient Joppa, seen
above the houses and alleys of the old town.

MY SHELTER

You are my refuge and defence;
guide me and lead me as you have promised.
Keep me safe from the trap that has been
set for me;
you are my shelter.
I place myself in your care.
You will save me, Lord;
you are a faithful God.

You hate those who worship false gods;
but I trust in you.
I will be glad and rejoice,
because of your constant love.
You see my suffering;
you know my trouble.
You have not let my enemies capture me;
you have kept me safe. . .

How wonderful are the good things
you keep for those who fear you!
How wonderful is what you do in the sight
of everyone,
protecting those who trust you.

From PSALM 31

A farm and fields in the Syrian desert near Aleppo.

IN GOD'S SAFE-KEEPING

Whoever goes to the Most High for safety,
whoever remains under the protection of the
Almighty,
can say to the Lord,
'You are my defender and protector!
You are my God; in you I trust.'

He will surely keep you safe from all hidden
dangers,
and from all deadly diseases.
He will cover you with his wings;
you will be safe under his care;
his faithfulness will protect and defend you.
You will not be afraid of dangers at night,
or of sudden attacks during the day,
of the plagues that strike in the dark,
or of the evils that kill in daylight.

From PSALM 91

On the road from Jerusalem to Jericho, formerly
notorious for bandits, and scene of Jesus' story of
the Good Samaritan.

WHEN I AM AFRAID

When I am afraid, O Most High,
I put my trust in you.
I trust in God and praise his promise;
in him I trust, and I will not be afraid.
What can mere man do to me?

You know how troubled I am;
you have kept a record of my tears.
Aren't they listed in your book?
The day I call to you,
my enemies will be turned back.
This I know—God is on my side!
I trust in God and praise his promise;
I will praise the promise of the Lord.
In him I trust, and I will not be afraid.
What can mere man do to me?
God, I will offer you what I have promised;
I will give you my offering of praise,
because you have rescued me from death
and kept me from defeat.
And so I walk in the presence of God,
in the light that shines on the living.

From PSALM 56

The sun seen through the branches of an acacia, one
of the few trees to grow in the desert.

WHEN I AM ANXIOUS

Lord, happy is the man whom you instruct,
the man to whom you teach your law,
to give him rest from days of trouble . . .

Who stood up for me against the wicked?
Who took my side against the evildoers?
If the Lord had not helped me,
I would have gone quickly to the land of
silence.
I said, 'I am falling';
but, Lord, your constant love held me up.
When I am anxious and worried,
you comfort me and make me glad.

From PSALM 94

A track through deep shadow in the mountains of
Samaria.

MY HELP COMES FROM THE LORD

I look to the mountains;
where will my help come from?
My help comes from the Lord,
who made heaven and earth.

May he not let me fall;
may my protector keep awake!
The protector of Israel
does not doze or sleep!
The Lord will guard you;
he is by your side to protect you.
The sun will not hurt you during the day,
nor the moon during the night.

The Lord will protect you from all danger;
he will keep you safe.
He will protect you as you come and go,
from now on and for ever.

PSALM 121

The moon over the mountains of Lebanon, still
streaked with snow in the late spring.

NEVER SHAKEN

Those who trust in the Lord are like Mount
Zion,
which can never be shaken, never be moved.
As the mountains surround Jerusalem,
so the Lord surrounds his people,
from now on and for ever.

From PSALM 125

On 'Mount Zion', the hill on which Jerusalem was
built, the walls of the ancient Temple area still stand
today.

GOD IS WITH US

God is our shelter and strength,
always ready to help in times of trouble.
So we will not be afraid, even if the earth is
shaken
and mountains fall into the ocean depths;
even if the seas roar and rage,
and the hills are shaken by the violence.

There is a river that brings joy to the city of
God,
to the sacred house of the Most High.
God lives in the city, and it will never be
destroyed;
at early dawn he will come to its help.
Nations are terrified, kingdoms are shaken;
God roars out, and the earth dissolves.

The Lord Almighty is with us;
the God of Jacob is our refuge!

From PSALM 46

Soon after its source, the River Jordan is already a
forceful, rushing stream.

TRUST IN HIM

Trust in the Lord and do good;
live in the land and be safe.
Seek your happiness with the Lord,
and he will give you what you most desire.

Give yourself to the Lord;
trust in him, and he will help you;
he will cause your goodness to shine as the
light
and your righteousness as the noonday sun.
Be calm before the Lord and wait patiently
for him to act;
don't be worried about those who prosper
or those who succeed in their evil plans . . .

Those who trust in the Lord will live safely
in the land,
but the wicked will be driven out.

From PSALM 37

In the streets of the old city of Jerusalem.

LORD, I LOOK UP TO YOU

Lord, I look up to you,
up to heaven, where you rule.
As the servant depends on his master,
and the maid depends on her mistress,
so we keep looking to you, Lord our God,
until you have mercy on us.

Be merciful to us, Lord, be merciful;
we have been treated with so much contempt!
We have been mocked too long by the rich,
and scorned by proud oppressors!

PSALM 123

Keeping the sheep on the stony slopes of a hill in
central Turkey, near ancient Lystra.

HEAR MY CRY

In my despair I call to you, Lord,
Hear my cry, Lord
listen to my call for help!
If you kept a record of our sins,
who could escape being condemned?
But you forgive us,
so that we should fear you.

I wait eagerly for the Lord's help,
and in his word I trust.
I wait for the Lord,
more eagerly than watchmen wait for the
dawn,
than watchmen wait for the dawn.

Israel, trust in the Lord,
because his love is constant,
and he is always willing to save.
He will save his people Israel
from all their sins.

From PSALM 130

Light on the waters of one of the sources of the
Jordan, at Caesarea Philippi in northern Israel.

IN OLD AGE

Lord, I am safe with you;
never let me be defeated!
Because you are righteous, help me and
rescue me.
Listen to me and save me!
Be my secure shelter,
and a strong fortress to protect me;
you are my refuge and defence . . .

My God, rescue me from wicked men,
from the power of cruel and evil men.
Lord, I put my hope in you;
I have trusted in you since I was young.
I have relied on you all my life;
you have protected me since I was born;
I will always praise you!

From PSALM 71

An old man watches the passers-by at Tsefat, Israel.

GOD'S WORD

Your word, Lord, will last for ever;
it is firm in heaven.
Your faithfulness endures through all the ages;
you have set the earth in place and it remains.
All things remain to this day because of your
command,
because they are all your servants.
If your law had not been the source of my joy,
I would have died from my punishment.
I will never neglect your rules,
because by them you have kept me alive.
I am yours – save me!
I have tried to obey your commands.
Wicked men are waiting to kill me,
but I will meditate on your laws.
I have learned that nothing is perfect;
but your commandment has no limits.

From PSALM 119

Standing stone in the Negev desert.

AT PEACE

Lord, I have given up my pride,
and turned from my arrogance.
I am not concerned with great matters,
or with subjects too difficult for me.
But I am content and at peace.
As a child lies quietly in its mother's arms,
so my heart is quiet within me.
Israel, trust in the Lord,
from now on and for ever!

PSALM 131

Flocks graze peacefully as the sun sets over the hills
of Galilee.